COMPANION WORKBOOK & STUDY GUIDE

Unshackle
YOUR
Wings

Cover design by Tessy Tanyi
Cover photo by Jenish

ISBN: 978-1-964794-77-8   1 2 3 4 5 6 7 8 9 10

Printed in the United States of America

Unshackle
YOUR
Wings

**DISCOVER YOUR TRUE IDENTITY
AND FULFILL YOUR DIVINE PURPOSE**

TESSY TANYI

Contents

INTRODUCTION *Your Souring Journey* 7

CHAPTER 1. *The Eagle's Reflection* 9

CHAPTER 2. *The Awakening* 14

CHAPTER 3. *Identity Crisis* 20

CHAPTER 4. *Unmasking Identity Thieves* 30

CHAPTER 5. *The Eagle Within You* 36

CHAPTER 6. *Reflect and Rise* 42

CHAPTER 7. *Wings of Change* 50

CHAPTER 8. *Preparing for the Flight Ahead* 55

CHAPTER 9. *Soaring with Purpose* 61

CHAPTER 10. *Weathering the Storm* 67

CHAPTER 11. *Associations* 74

CHAPTER 12. *The Eagle's Gaze* 80

CHAPTER 13. *Rise Above the Battle* 85

CHAPTER 14. *Feeding the Eagle Within* 89

CHAPTER 15. *The Wilderness Experience* 94

CHAPTER 16. *From Hidden to Heralded* 99

CHAPTER 17. *The Majestic Eagle* 105

CHAPTER 18. *Final Charge* 111

Your Souring Journey

This isn't just a study—it's a spiritual flight school. Each chapter trains a different aspect of your divine design, transforming you from grounded to glory-bound.

THE EAGLE'S TRANSFORMATION PATH:

CHAPTER 1: THE EAGLE'S REFLECTION
Focus: Correct your self-perception

Distinction: Foundations of identity (who God says you are)

CHAPTER 2: THE AWAKENING
Focus: Break invisible cages

Distinction: Liberation from mental/emotional limits

CHAPTER 3: IDENTITY CRISIS
Focus: Resurrect buried purpose

Distinction: Turn potential into action

CHAPTER 6: REFLECT AND RISE
Focus: Turn stagnation into momentum

Distinction: Bridge between identity and activation

CHAPTER 7: WINGS OF CHANGE
Focus: Shatter man-made boxes

Distinction: External lifestyle shift

CHAPTER 10: WEATHERING THE STORM

Focus: Grow through adversity

Distinction: Pressure-test your faith

CHAPTER 12: THE EAGLE'S GAZE

Focus: Develop spiritual vision

Distinction: See as heaven sees

CHAPTER 15: THE WILDERNESS EXPERIENCE

Focus: Thrive in preparation seasons

Distinction: Divine delay ≠ divine denial

FINAL CHARGE (CHAPTER 18)

Focus: Launch into destiny

Distinction: Your "flight manual" for lifelong soaring

HOW TO USE THIS WORKBOOK:

- **Personal Growth:** *Complete exercises sequentially for full transformation.*
- **Group Study:** *Use discussion questions to sharpen one another (iron sharpens iron).*
- **Daily Reinforcement:** *Revisit declarations and trackers to maintain altitude.*

YOUR INVITATION:

This is your summons to trade earthbound thinking for sky-high living. The wind of the Spirit is stirring—will you spread your wings?

The Eagle's Reflection

SEEING YOURSELF THROUGH GOD'S EYES

"Who do you see when you look in the mirror?"

INTRODUCTION: MIRROR OR MASTERPIECE?
CHOOSING HOW YOU SEE YOURSELF

KEY VERSE

"I praise you because I am fearfully and wonderfully made; your works are wonderful, I know that full well."

—Psalm 139:14 (NIV)

This chapter will help you:

- **Spot** *false self-perceptions (world's vs. God's mirror)*
- **Swap** *lies for Scripture-truth (Psalm 139:14, Ephesians 2:10)*
- **List** *three societal/family-imposed limitations*
- **Write** *a divine identity letter (Ephesians 2:10)*
- **Craft** *personalized "I Am" affirmations*
- **Practice** *seven days of spoken declarations*
- **Surrender** *one limiting belief in prayer*

RESULT: A ROCK-SOLID, BIBLICAL SELF-IMAGE AND DAILY TOOLS TO LIVE AS GOD'S MASTERPIECE.

ILLUSTRATION

Remember the lion raised among sheep? (See Unshackle Your Wings: Discover Your True Identity and Fulfill Your Divine Purpose, Chapter 1, Page 24). This mirrors how we adopt false identities.

QUESTION TO PONDER:

Revisit that powerful parable as you reflect on your own false identities. What "false reflection" have you believed about yourself?

_____

_____

_____

_____

SECTION 1: THE MIRRORS WE CHOOSE

CARNIVAL MIRROR VS. GOD'S MIRROR
Use the two columns below:

CARNIVAL MIRROR (DISTORTIONS)	GOD'S MIRROR (TRUTHS)

SCRIPTURE DIVE: JAMES 1:23-24

How does God's Word correct our self-image?

_____

_____

_____

_____

_____

PERSONAL REFLECTION

When you look in the mirror, what words come to mind?

_____

_____

_____

_____

_____

Describe a time you felt you didn't measure up.

_____

_____

_____

_____

_____

SECTION 2: THE LION'S REFLECTION

UNPACKING FALSE NARRATIVES

List 3 beliefs shaped by society/family:

- _____
- _____
- _____

How is God's Word a "true mirror" (James 1:23-24)?

_____

_____

_____

_____

FAITH IN ACTION

Letter from God: *Write as if God is speaking to you (use Ephesians 2:10).*

Dear _____,

_____

_____

_____

_____

_____

_____

_____

_____

Love,
Your Heavenly Father

SECTION 3: REFRAMING YOUR PERSPECTIVE

"I Am" Affirmations (Example: "I am God's masterpiece"):

- _____
- _____
- _____

CHALLENGE: *Say these aloud daily for a week!*

OPTIONAL GROUP DISCUSSION GUIDE ///////////////////////////////////

- *Which "bar" of your cage (from Section 1) felt most relatable? Why?*
- *How did the "Letter from God" exercise challenge your false narratives?*
- *Which "I Am" affirmation felt hardest to believe? What would it look like to live it out?*

NEXT STEPS (OPTIONAL):

GROUP CHALLENGE:
Pair up and share one "key" (from Section 1) you'll focus on this week.

CLOSING PRAYER ///////////////////////////////////

"Lord, help me see myself as You do. Amen."

FINAL REFLECTION ///////////////////////////////////

One limiting belief I'll release to make room for growth:

_____

_____

_____

_____

The Awakening

BREAKING FREE FROM THE CAGE

*"You were born for open skies, yet many
live in cages they don't recognize."*

INTRODUCTION: CAGE OR SKY?—CHOOSING YOUR TERRITORY //////////////

This chapter is a companion guide to breaking free from your cage. It will help you:

- **Identify** *your "cage" (limiting beliefs, fears, false identities)*
- **Recognize** *the bars (e.g., "I'm too old") and locks (e.g., others' opinions) holding you back*
- **Discover** *your hidden "key" (truths/resources to break free)*
- **Evaluate** *costs of freedom (relationships/habits to change)*
- **Rewrite** *three "chicken mentality" lies into eagle declarations (e.g., "I am God's chosen voice")*
- **Create** *a three-step Flight Plan with deadlines (action, relationship, fear to confront)*
- **Craft** *a twenty-word "Skywriting Prayer" declaration of identity*
- **Commit** *to weekly growth checkpoints*

RESULT: A PERSONALIZED ROADMAP TO BREAK FREE FROM LIMITATIONS AND START LIVING IN BOLD, GOD-GIVEN FREEDOM.

SECTION 1: RECOGNIZING YOUR CAGE

"You cannot escape what you don't recognize."

THE MIRROR EXERCISE
What limitations did you notice you have accepted as normal?

- ❑ *Fear of failure*
- ❑ *Others' expectations*
- ❑ *Past mistakes*
- ❑ *Age limitations*
- ❑ *Write your own:* _____

CAGE IDENTIFICATION
"My personal cage is built with:"

- *Bars of:*_____*(e.g., "I'm too old")*
- *Locked by:* _____*(e.g., "Others' opinions")*
- *Key hidden in:* _____*(e.g., "My faith in God's timing")*

The key isn't lost—it's already within reach but requires intentional discovery.

SCRIPTURE REFLECTION (JEREMIAH 1:5)
How does God's foreknowledge of you challenge your self-limitations?

_____

_____

_____

SECTION 2: THE COST OF FREEDOM

*"Every eagle must choose between the safety
of the cage or the freedom of the sky."*

SEPARATION INVENTORY

Circle what may need to change as you awaken:

RELATIONSHIPS	HABITS	ENVIRONMENTS	THOUGHT PATTERNS
NEGATIVE FRIENDS	SCROLLING	TOXIC WORKPLACE	"I CAN'T" STATEMENTS
UNSUPPORTIVE FAMILY	COMPLACENCY	COMFORT ZONES	COMPARING MYSELF

BOLDNESS CHALLENGE

Complete this sentence:

"I will stop waiting for _____'s permission to_____."

SECTION 3: OWNING YOUR EAGLE IDENTITY

"You don't learn to soar—you remember how."

DIVINE ENCOUNTER JOURNAL

Describe a moment you felt God calling you higher:

- *Vision/dream*
  Details:_____

- *Scripture that "spoke" to you*
  Details: _____

- *Unexplainable hunger for more*
  Details: _____

ANTI-CHICKEN MANIFESTO

Rewrite 3 "chicken mentality" statements as eagle declarations:

1) "I'm just a_____" > "I am God's_____." (John 15:16)

2) "It's too late for me_____" > "My time is_____." (Joel 2:25)

3) "I don't have what it takes_____" > "I carry_____." (2 Timothy 1:7)

DECLARE & DO CHALLENGE

TODAY'S MISSION:
Pick one declaration and act on it. If you wrote "I am God's voice," share encouragement with someone. If you wrote "My time is now," take one step toward a delayed dream.

SECTION 4: SPREADING YOUR WINGS 〰〰〰〰〰〰〰〰〰〰〰〰〰〰〰〰〰〰〰〰

"Soaring begins when you stop calculating risks and start trusting your wings."

FLIGHT PLAN: DIVINE INSTRUCTION FOR SOARING
"Those who hope in the Lord will renew their strength. They will soar on wings like eagles. . . ." (Isaiah 40:31)

Your first 3 in-flight instructions from God:

1) ACTION TO TAKE
"What practical step is God asking you to obey?" (Example: "Apply for the leadership program.")

_____

Deadline: _____ *(give an exact date)*

2) RELATIONSHIP TO ADDRESS
"Who does God want you to forgive, encourage, or reconcile with?"

_____

(Example: "Call my sister to heal our rift.")
Deadline: _____

3) FEAR TO CONFRONT

"What fear has grounded you? Name it and claim God's promise over it."

_____

(Example: "Fear of rejection—I am accepted in Christ (Ephesians 1:6).")
Deadline: _____

POST-FLIGHT CHECK-IN *(Optional but powerful for accountability)*
"After each deadline, journal: How did obedience strengthen your wings?"

SKYWRITING PRAYER

Write a 20-word declaration over your life (like the angel's message):

Example:
"I AM God's unstoppable voice, armed with love, walking in miracles, and destined to lead nations to His light."

Now, write yours:

"I AM_____

_____

_____

(Count your words—make every one powerful!)

WEEKLY CHECKPOINTS

(For ongoing transformation)

WEEK	FOCUS	EVIDENCE OF GROWTH
1	IDENTIFYING CAGES	NOTICED 3 LIMITING BELIEFS
2	PRACTICING FLIGHT	TOOK 1 BOLD ACTION
3	EAGLE COMMUNITY	CONNECTED WITH_____

SOAR COMMITMENT

"I, _____, choose to awaken daily by_____. When fear arises, I will_____.
My liftoff date is_____."

Signature: _____Date:_____

Identity Crisis

CREATED FOR GREATNESS

"You carry resurrection power in your bones—don't bury it with the dead."

INTRODUCTION: GRAVE OR GROUNDBREAKING? —RESURRECTING YOUR PURPOSE

"The greatest tragedy isn't death—it's the potential buried while you're still alive."

This interactive workbook is designed to help you discover and walk in your God-given identity. Through reflection questions, Scripture studies, and practical exercises, you'll:

- **Confront** *"cemetery thinking" (unlived potential) through legacy visualization*
- **Rewrite** *your life narrative with an eight-word epitaph and urgent action step*
- **Challenge** *stagnation with "What If?" scenarios (biblical + personal)*
- **Detox** *false labels using Scripture (Ephesians 2:10, 1 Peter 2:9)*
- **Bury** *false identities with a symbolic funeral and Scripture missiles*
- **Align** *with biblical heroes' transformations (Moses, Rahab, Peter)*
- **Activate** *purpose through twenty-one-day declarations and thirty-day identity experiments*
- **Leverage** *community insight to confirm gifts/callings*

RESULT: A CLEAR, ACTIONABLE BLUEPRINT TO REPLACE IDENTITY CRISIS WITH GOD-GIVEN CONFIDENCE AND PURPOSE.

SECTION 1: THE CEMETERY OF UNLIVED POTENTIAL

KEY CONCEPT

"The cemetery holds authors who never wrote, singers who never sang, and people who died with wings but never flew."

REFLECTION EXERCISES:

1) Legacy Visualization
Your life is a letter written to the world. What will it say?

Epitaph of Purpose
Imagine your funeral. What eight-word epitaph captures your life's impact?*
Example: She loved fiercely and ignited others' destinies.
Your turn:

_____

_____

The Unwritten Regret
What would devastate you if left undone?
Example: I played it safe and left my dreams dormant.
Your turn:

_____

_____

Legacy Bridge
Now, write one action today that moves you from regret to epitaph:
I will _____ *by* _____.

2) *"What If" History Challenge*

Biblical "What if?"
What if Moses had stayed a shepherd?
Example: God's people might have died in slavery.
Your answer:

_____

_____

Personal "What if?"
What if I never pursue my dream of _____
Example: Generations could miss the hope God placed in me.
Your answer:

_____

_____

Personal "What if?"
The world needs my unique gift of _____
Example: Bold creativity to solve problems in my community.
Your answer:

_____

_____

3) *Potential Inventory*

What untapped strengths is God calling you to activate?

1) Ability: _____ (Example: public speaking)
   Next step: _____ *(e.g., volunteer to teach Sunday school)*

2) Ability: _____
   Next step: _____

3) Ability: _____
   Next step: _____

SECTION 2: IDENTITY FOUNDATIONS

KEY CONCEPT

*"You can't know what you're capable
of until you know who you are."*

BIBLICAL IDENTITY ASSESSMENT:

1) Label Detox

Step 1: *List five identity labels you currently wear (roles, struggles, or stereotypes):*
Examples: perfectionist, people-pleaser, broken

1. _____
2. _____
3. _____
4. _____
5. _____

Step 2: *Put a ＊ next to any label NOT found in Scripture*

2) Manufacturer's Manual

God's Word defines you. Rewrite your labels below using these verses:

EPHESIANS 2:10: *I am God's _____ , created for _____.*

1 PETER 2:9: *I am a _____ , called to proclaim _____.*

JEREMIAH 1:5: *Before I was born, God appointed me to _____.*

3) The John the Baptist Test (John 1:19-22)

False Title: *I've believed I'm just a _____.*
True Confession: *But Scripture says I am _____.*

SECTION 3: FROM CRISIS TO CLARITY

KEY CONCEPT

"An identity crisis is the collision between who you've believed you are and who God says you are. It is the soul's invitation to exchange your mirror (self-perception) for God's microscope (His design)."

TRANSFORMATION EXERCISES:

1) False Identity Funeral

Step 1: *Write a eulogy for your false self (be brutally honest):*

Dear [False Identity],

You told me I was _____. But Scripture says I'm _____. Today, I bury you in Jesus' name.

Signed,

[Your True Name in Christ]

Step 2: *Arm yourself with three Scripture missiles to destroy this lie:*

1. Verse: _____ (e.g., Romans 8:1)
   Truth Declared: "I am _____."
2. Verse: _____
   Truth Declared: "I am _____."
3. Verse: _____
   Truth Declared: "I am _____."

2) Biblical Case Studies

Even heroes faced identity battles—but God rewrote their stories. Complete this table:

BIBLICAL FIGURE	THEIR CRISIS	GOD'S TRUTH	YOUR PARALLEL
MOSES	"I CAN'T SPEAK"	"I WILL BE WITH YOUR MOUTH" (EXODUS 4:12)	MY _____ IS WHERE GOD'S POWER SHOWS UP STRONGEST.
RAHAB	"I'M JUST A PROSTITUTE"	"INCLUDED IN CHRIST'S LINEAGE" (MATTHEW 1:5)	GOD IS USING MY PAST TO _____.
PETER	"I DENIED JESUS"	"FEED MY SHEEP" (JOHN 21:17)	MY GREATEST FAILURE IS NOW MY ASSIGNMENT TO _____.

3) Obedience Experiment

Step 1: *This week, I will obey God in this "small thing":*

I will _____ by _____ [date].
(Example: Apologize to my coworker by Friday.)

Step 2: *Post-obedience journal prompt:*

How did this act of obedience . . .

Expose a lie I believed about myself?

_____

_____

Confirm a purpose I'd overlooked?

_____

_____

KEY CONCEPT

"Greatness isn't achieved—it's remembered. Live today in light of how you want to be remembered tomorrow."

ACTIVATION TOOLS:

1) Daily Identity Declarations
Your words shape your reality. Craft three battle cries based on:

Who God says you are (e.g., I am God's masterpiece (Ephesians 2:10), fully equipped for my assignment):
Your turn: I am _____

_____

What He's called you to do (e.g., I reconcile broken relationships as a peacemaker; Matthew 5:9):
Your turn: I _____

_____

How He sees your future (e.g., My faithfulness will ignite generational change; Acts 13:36):
Your turn: My life will _____

_____

2) Passion Resurrection
What dream have you buried under "someday" or "impossible"?

Buried dream: I once wanted to _____ *but stopped*
because _____.

Resurrection step (this month):
I will _____ *by* _____ *[date].*
(Example: Email a local writer's group by Friday.)

3) Community Mirror

Others often see your purpose before you do. Ask three trusted people:

"When do you see me most alive?" (record responses) _____

_____

- *I light up when* _____.
- *I'm unstoppable doing* _____.

"What unique gift do I bring?" (record responses) _____

_____

"I am the kind of person who?" (record responses) _____

_____

Action Step: *Circle one repeated theme—then lean into it this week.*

SECTION 5: LIFETIME CHALLENGE ~~~~~~~~~~~~~~~~~~~~~~~~~~~~~~~~

KEY CONCEPT

*"Don't die with your song still inside you—
the world needs your God-given melody."*

THE THIRTY-DAY IDENTITY EXPERIMENT

1) Morning Routine (five minutes):

Scripture Fuel:
Read one identity verse aloud (e.g., Ephesians 2:10). Circle the phrase that stirs your heart.
Today's Verse: _____

Identity Declaration:

Today I live as God's _____ *[biblical identity], doing*

_____ *[purpose action].*

(Example: Today I live as God's ambassador [2 Cor. 5:20], restoring broken relationships.)

2) Evening Reflection (seven minutes):

Victory Spotting:

Where did I mirror my true identity today? _____

_____

(Example: Spoke encouragement—that's my gift as a builder-upper.)

Today's Win: _____.

Lie Exposure:

Where did I shrink back? _____

_____

(Example: Avoided leading because I called myself "unqualified.")

Today's Growth: _____.

3) Legacy Builder:

Do one thing weekly that only YOU can do—leverage your unique design.

This Week's Action: *I will* _____

_____ *by* _____ *[date].*

(Example: Record my testimony to share with my small group.)

CLOSING DECLARATION

"I renounce every label not stamped by Heaven. I am not my past. Not my job. Not their opinions. I am God's masterpiece (Ephesians 2:10), armed with purpose, forged for this moment in history. Today, I shed counterfeit identities and rise into my royal calling. My potential will not be buried. My wings are unshackled. I SOAR."

Signed: _____ *Date* _____

Witnessed by: _____

KEY NEXT STEPS:

- ***Tear and Post:*** *Display your declaration on your mirror/wallet.*
- ***Small Group:*** *Discuss breakthroughs using: "Where did you see your true identity this week?"*
- ***Quarterly Check-In:*** *Revisit this guide every ninety days to track growth.*
- ***#CreatedForGreatness:*** *Share your journey to inspire others.*

Final Tip: *When doubts arise, point to your signed declaration and say: "This is my legal identity in Christ."*

CLOSING PRAYER

Father,

I thank You that I was created for greatness—not by accident, but with eternal intention. Let me walk boldly in the identity You've written over me. Awaken me to the divine assignments hiding in ordinary days. Help me to soar—one obedient step at a time. Amen.

Unmasking Identity Thieves

BREAKING FREE FROM PERSONAL LIES AND FALSE LABELS

INTRODUCTION

This isn't just a workbook—it's a freedom journey. This chapter will help you:

- **Detect** *three to five "identity thieves" sabotaging your self-worth (shame, comparison, past failures)*
- **Armor** *up with specific Scripture weapons to dismantle each lie*
- **Conduct** *a spiritual "identity theft report" to trace lies to your source*
- **Rewrite** *your personal narrative with God's courtroom declarations*
- **Activate** *a seven-day truth bombardment plan to reprogram your mindset*

RESULT: A LIBERATED IDENTITY, ARMED WITH UNSHAKABLE TRUTH AND PRACTICAL DEFENSE STRATEGIES AGAINST FUTURE ATTACKS.

BEFORE YOU BEGIN:

Father, rip off every mask the enemy has placed on me. Show me who You say I am—no filters, no lies.

Pause here. Listen. Write any impressions.

_____

_____

_____

_____

SECTION 1: RECOGNIZING YOUR IDENTITY THIEVES

KEY CONCEPT

"The thief's voice shouts; God's truth whispers. Which will you amplify? (John 10:10)"

EXERCISE 1: IDENTITY THIEF AUDIT

List three to five "criminals" that have stolen your true self (e.g., shame, perfectionism, others' opinions):

    1. Name: _____ (Example: People-Pleaser)

      Lie It Tells: "I must earn love by performing."

    2. Name: _____

      Lie It Tells: _____

    3. Name: _____

      Lie It Tells: _____

    4. Name: _____

      Lie It Tells: _____

    5. Name: _____

      Lie It Tells: _____

REFLECTION

Which thief has been running your life? How? _____

_____

_____

_____

_____

EXERCISE 2: THE EAGLE VS. CHICKEN TEST

Chicken Mode: *I've been acting like a chicken in* _____
by _____ .

Eagle Shift: *To soar, I will* _____
_____ *starting today.*

SECTION 2: GOD'S MEASUREMENT OF SUCCESS

KEY CONCEPT

"Man looks at résumés; God reads hearts (1 Samuel 16:7)."

EXERCISE 3: SUCCESS SMACKDOWN

WORLD'S DEFINITION	GOD'S DEFINITION
MORE FOLLOWERS	MORE FAITHFULNESS

GUT CHECK:
What worldly measure do you need to quit chasing?
I'll stop obsessing over _____ *and*
start pursuing _____ .

EXERCISE 4: LEGACY REWIND

Imagine your heavenly homecoming. God says:
"Well done! I cheered loudest when you _____

_____

_____

SECTION 3: ACTIVATING YOUR TREASURE

KEY TRUTH

Your "junk" is God's raw material for miracles (2 Corinthians 4:7).

EXERCISE 5: TREASURE MAP

1) **Buried Gift:** *I've neglected my ability to* _____

_____

_____

2) **Digging Plan:** *This month, I'll* _____

_____

to revive it.

EXERCISE 6: THE "RAHAB" PRINCIPLE

Like Rahab, your past doesn't disqualify you—it equips you.

Past struggle to superpower: My _____ *now helps me*

_____ *.*

SECTION 4: DAILY FREEDOM PRACTICES

EXERCISE 7: MIRROR MANIFESTO

Write three Scripture-based declarations (e.g., "I am fearfully and wonderfully made," Psalm 139:14):

1) **Morning Battle Cry:** *"I am* _____.
2) **Midday Reminder:** *"I carry* _____.
3) **Evening Truth:** *"My life matters because* _____.

CHALLENGE: SAY THESE WHILE STARING INTO YOUR EYES FOR TWENTY-ONE DAYS.

EXERCISE 8: PAUL'S REBOOT

Complete this transformation timeline:

OLD IDENTITY (SAUL)	NEW TRUTH (PAUL)	FIRST STEP
PERSECUTOR	APOSTLE	PREACH CHRIST

CLOSING IDENTITY PACT

Read aloud, sign, and post where you'll see it daily:

Today, I burn every fake ID issued by:
    My past _____
    People _____
    The enemy's lie that _____

I am officially:
    Name: _____
    Purpose: _____

Signed: _____ *Date:*_____
Witness: _____

NEXT STEPS:

- **Text one declaration** *to a friend right now.*
- **Monthly Checkup:** *Revisit Section 4 every thirty days.*
- **Lie Detector:** *When doubts hit, shout: "Case closed! I'm* _____*!"*

The Eagle Within You

YOUR TRUE IDENTITY

"You're not learning to soar—you're remembering how."

INTRODUCTION: YOUR SPIRITUAL FLIGHT SCHOOL

This chapter will help you:

- **Diagnose** *areas of "chicken mentality" (playing small, fear-based living)*
- **Activate** *eagle vision through Isaiah 40:31 meditation and perspective shifts*
- **Declare** *three personalized "I Am" statements rooted in Scripture*
- **Identify** *three ways you've blended in when called to stand out*
- **Launch** *a ninety-day "Flight Plan" with specific obedience steps*
- **Build** *an "Eagle Squad" of like-minded believers for accountability*

RESULT: A PRACTICAL TRANSFORMATION FROM SURVIVAL MODE TO SOARING IN GOD-GIVEN AUTHORITY, WITH CLEAR METRICS FOR GROWTH.

PRE-FLIGHT PRAYER

Spirit of God, strip away every lie that's clipped my wings. Awaken my true identity—show me what You see when You look at me.

Pause. Write what comes to mind:

_____

_____

_____

_____

_____

SECTION 1: EAGLE DIAGNOSTIC

KEY TRUTH

Chicken life is optional (Isaiah 40:31).

EXERCISE 1: GROUND AUDIT

I've been pecking dirt in these areas when called to soar:
   Example: Playing small in leadership to avoid criticism.
   Your Turn: _____

_____

EXERCISE 2: WING WEIGHTS

List three things tethering you to earth:

1) *Fear:* _____ *(e.g., Fear of rejection)*
2) *Habit:* _____ *(e.g., People-pleasing)*
3) *Lie:* _____ *(e.g., I'm not ready)*

Prophetic Push: *Circle one to surrender today.*

SECTION 2: EAGLE VISION TRAINING

KEY INSIGHT

Eagles see storms as updrafts.

EXERCISE 3: LENS UPGRADE

NATURAL SIGHT (PROBLEM)	EAGLE VISION (OPPORTUNITY)
CONFLICT AT WORK	CHANCE TO MODEL GRACE

SCRIPTURE REWRITE

Paraphrase Isaiah 40:31 as a personal promise:

When I _____, God will _____.

SECTION 3: BOLDNESS BOOTCAMP

KEY TRUTH

Timidity is amnesia of your Spirit-filled identity (2 Timothy 1:7).

EXERCISE 4: COURAGE SPOTLIGHT

Timid Area: *I shrink back from* _____.

Bold Action (This Week): *I will* _____
by _____ *[date].*

EAGLE DECLARATIONS:

1) I am **uncontainable**—*filled with the Spirit's fullness.*
2) I walk in **authority** *over fear and intimidation.*
3) I am **equipped** *to* _____

SECTION 4: LEAVING THE FLOCK

KEY INSIGHT

Barnyards breed conformity; skies demand uniqueness.

EXERCISE 5: DISTINCTION CHECK

Three ways I've blended in:
Voice: _____ *(e.g., Staying silent on hard truths)*
Style: _____ *(e.g., Copying others' calling)*
Vision: _____ *(e.g., Lowering goals to fit in)*

Soaring Shift: *This week, I'll stand out by* _____
_____

KEY TRUTH

*Eagles don't flock—you find them
one at a time in high places.*

EXERCISE 6: ALTITUDE SCAN

SOARING AREAS	GROUNDED AREAS
PRAYER LIFE	PUBLIC SPEAKING

God's Nudge: *He's saying: "Let go of* _____
to seize _____ *."*

EXERCISE 7: FLIGHT PLAN

Ninety-Day Goal: _____ *(e.g., Launch mentorship program)*

_____

First Step: _____ *(e.g., Outline curriculum by Friday)*

_____

Co-Pilot: _____ *(Accountability partner's name)*

FINAL DECLARATION: THE SKY MANIFESTO

Read aloud, sign, and post where you'll see it daily:

I am done with domesticated living.
I renounce:

> *The fear of* _____
> *The lie that* _____

I declare:

- *My wings are renewed (Isaiah 40:31)*
- *My vision is clear (Ephesians 1:18)*
- *My destiny is skies, not earth (Colossians 3:2)*

Sign Your Name: _____*Date:*_____
Witnessed By: _____

NEXT STEPS

- **Daily:** Recite your Eagle Declarations during morning routines.
- **Weekly:** Text your co-pilot one soaring victory.
- **Monthly:** Revisit your Flight Plan and adjust altitude.

Reflect and Rise

THE PATH UPWARD BEGINS WITH LOOKING INWARD

*"You can't rise higher than the lies
you're willing to confront."*

INTRODUCTION: THE COURAGE TO LOOK

This chapter will help you:

- **Spot** *where you've settled for less than God's best*
- **Shift** *from frustration to purpose in waiting seasons*
- **Mine** *past failures for growth insights*
- **Build** *a ninety-day action plan with deadlines*
- **Write** *a "Liftoff Declaration" to lock in commitment*
- **Track** *progress with weekly/monthly checkpoints*

RESULT: FROM PASSIVE REFLECTION TO PURPOSEFUL ACTION—EQUIPPED TO RISE FROM STAGNATION TO SOARING.

PRE-REFLECTION PRAYER:

Father, strip away my defenses. Show me:

1) *Where I've hidden behind* _____

2) *Where I've striven in* _____

3) *Where You're calling me to* _____

Write His whispers below:

_____

_____

_____

_____

SECTION 1: GROUND CHECK

KEY TRUTH

Settling is self-sabotage disguised as contentment (Lamentations 3:40).

EXERCISE 1: SETTLEMENT SCAN

I've accepted "good enough" in these areas when God promised "more than":
Example: Staying in a joyless job because it's safe.

Your Turn:

_____

_____

_____

EXERCISE 2: PATTERN AUTOPSY

What fuels this stagnation?

BEHAVIOR	THOUGHT LIE	FEAR BENEATH
PROCRASTINATION	"I'LL FAIL ANYWAY"	BEING EXPOSED AS INADEQUATE

Lightbulb Moment: *Circle one fear to confront this week.*

SECTION 2: BREAKING MUNDANITY 〰〰〰〰〰〰〰〰〰〰〰〰〰

KEY INSIGHT

Routine is either a runway or a rut.

EXERCISE 3: CYCLE INTERRUPTION

I keep repeating _____
when I know _____.

(Example: Skipping prayer, then wondering why I feel empty.)

EXERCISE 4: FIRE AUDIT

I traded passion for comfort when I _____.

Rebuild Plan: *To reignite this area, I'll* _____.

_____

SECTION 3: THE HONESTY IMPERATIVE ///////////////////////////

KEY TRUTH

Your breakthroughs live in the shadows you avoid.

EXERCISE 5: FEAR INVENTORY

Three obedience delays and their roots:

Avoiding _____
because _____.

Postponing _____
due to _____.

Ignoring _____
fearing _____.

EXERCISE 6: JEREMIAH 29:11 REWRITE

I resist asking for help with _____
because _____.

SECTION 4: HUMILITY = FUEL ///////////////////////////////////

KEY CONCEPT

Pride checks progress at the door.

EXERCISE 7: HELP HESITATION

I resist asking for help with _____
because _____.

EXERCISE 8: FAILURE REFRAME

What I called a failure in _____ *was actually*
God teaching me _____.

SECTION 5: RISE LAUNCH

KEY INSIGHT

Reflection without action is self-improvement theater.

EXERCISE 9: DREAM DEFIB

I've suppressed this dream because _____:

Dream: _____
_____
_____

EXERCISE 10: OBEDIENCE KICKSTART

Within seventy-two hours, I will _____
to activate this dream.

FINAL DECLARATION: THE RISE MANIFESTO

Sign and date this contract with your future self:

I renounce:

   The lie that _____.

   The comfort of _____.

I embrace:

   Radical honesty about _____.

   Daily obedience in _____.

Sign Your Name: _____*Date:*_____

Witness: _____

NEXT STEPS:

- **Daily:** Complete the "Seven-Day Rise Challenge" (below)
- **Accountability:** Text your witness with one obedience win each Friday
- **Monthly:** Revisit your manifesto to assess altitude

SEVEN-DAY RISE CHALLENGE

SMALL ACTS OF OBEDIENCE CREATE BIG BREAKTHROUGHS.

Day 1: Truth Bomb

❑ *Identify one lie you've believed (from Chapter 6)*

❑ *Replace it with: "God says I am* _____ *"*

Day 2: Comfort Interrupt

❑ *Do one thing differently today (e.g., take a new route, speak up in a meeting)*

❑ *Journal: How did this disrupt autopilot?* _____

Day 3: Fear Facing

❏ *Take one step toward what you've avoided (e.g., send that email, make the call)*

❏ *Text your witness: "I did _____ today!"*

Day 4: Humility Flex

❏ *Ask for help with: _____*

❏ *Note the result: "I learned _____ "*

Day 5: Dream Fuel

❏ *Spend ten minutes researching/praying about your buried dream*

❏ *Write next step: _____*

Day 6: Obedience Test

❏ *Say "no" to: _____ (distraction/comparison)*

❏ *Say "yes" to: _____ (growth opportunity)*

Day 7: Soaring Declaration

❏ *Shout your manifesto aloud (Chapter 5)*

❏ *Post where you'll see it daily:* ❏ *Fridge* ❏ *Mirror* ❏ *Lock screen*

TRACK YOUR RISE
Your obedience is your altitude meter.

Wins This Week:

1. _____

2. _____

3. _____

What Surprised Me:

_____

_____

_____

One Habit to Keep:

_____

_____

_____

Witness Check-In:

This week, I broke through in _____. *My*
next step is _____.
(Text this to your witness by Sunday!)

CHAPTER 7

Wings of Change

NO MORE BOXES. ONLY WINGS.

*"The moment you stop trying to fit in
is the moment you begin to soar."*

INTRODUCTION: YOUR BREAKTHROUGH BLUEPRINT

This chapter will help you:

- **Identify** *three "boxes" (man-made limitations) holding you back*
- **Rewrite** *man-made labels into God-given truths (Ephesians 2:10)*
- **Activate** *a twenty-one-day "Wing Stretching Challenge"*
- **Replace** *fear-based decisions with faith-fueled risks*
- **Build** *a "Sky Squad" of like-minded soarers*

RESULT: A LIFE UNCONTAINED BY HUMAN EXPECTATIONS—LIVING FULLY IN GOD-DESIGNED FREEDOM AND PURPOSE

PRE-FLIGHT PRAYER:

Spirit of God, shatter every box I've been squeezed into. Give me the courage to stretch my wings—even if it scares me.

Pause. Write what comes to mind:

_____

_____

_____

_____

SECTION 1: BOX ARCHAEOLOGY

KEY TRUTH

Labels are lies with Velcro backing —
they stick until you rip them off.

EXERCISE 1: BOX ORIGINS

These voices told me I couldn't be _____:
Example: My third-grade teacher said I'd never write well.

Your Turn:

_____

_____

EXERCISE 2: LABELS EXCAVATION

Three false identities you've worn:

1) *I'm just a* _____ *(e.g., screw-up)*
2) *I'll never* _____ *(e.g., be free from this fear)*
3) *They said I'm* _____ *(e.g., too loud to lead)*

Lightbulb Moment: *Star the label that hurts most.*

SECTION 2: BOX DEMOLITION

KEY INSIGHT

Your wings work better outside the box.

EXERCISE 3: TRUTH RECLAMATION

LIE BELIEVED	GOD'S TRUTH	SCRIPTURE ANCHOR
"I'M UNWORTHY"	"I AM CHOSEN"	1 PETER 2:9

EXERCISE 4: ISAIAH 43:18-19 REWRITE

God is saying to me: "Stop staring at _____ *. Watch as I create* _____ *!"*

SECTION 3: WING STRETCHING

KEY TRUTH

Transformation isn't pretty—but flying is worth the awkward flapping.

EXERCISE 5: NEW YOU CELEBRATION

I'm stepping into my identity as a _____ *who* _____ *.*
(Example: A bold voice who liberates others)

EXERCISE 6: SHRINKING SPOT

I've been playing small in _____
when God says _____.

SECTION 4: DIVINE RHYTHM

KEY SCRIPTURE

"There's a season to nest, and a season to soar" (Ecclesiastes 3:1).

EXERCISE 7: SEASON SENSOR

Current Season: ❏ *Preparation*   ❏ *Launch*   ❏ *Storm*   ❏ *Harvest*

God's whisper: Stop rushing _____.
Embrace _____.

EXERCISE 8: SOAR SIGNAL

The Spirit is nudging me to _____
by _____.
(Example: Start that podcast by recording one episode)

SECTION 5: SPEAKING LIFE

KEY DECLARATION

Your words assign your wings their weight limit.

EXERCISE 9: IDENTITY AFFIRMATIONS

4) I am _____ (Ephesians 2:10).
5) I carry _____ (2 Timothy 1:7).
6) My wings are made for _____ (Isaiah 40:31).

Challenge: *Shout these over your morning coffee for twenty-one days.*

FINAL DECLARATION: WINGS MANIFESTO

Sign, date, and post where you'll see it daily:

I renounce:
- *The box of* _____
- *The lie that* _____

I declare:
- *My wingspan is* _____ *(your God-given purpose)*
- *My flight path is guided, not guessed (Proverbs 3:5–6)*

Sign Your Name: _____ Date: _____
Witness _____

NEXT STEPS:

- **Daily:** *Recite one declaration during your commute*
- **Weekly:** *Text your witness one "wing stretch" victory*
- **Monthly:** *Revisit Section 4 to check your season*

Preparing for the Flight Ahead

"Even eagles must prepare before they soar."

INTRODUCTION

This chapter will help you:

- **Audit** *your spiritual "flight readiness" in five key areas*
- **Identify** *three "weight triggers" that hinder altitude*
- **Develop** *a forty-day conditioning plan (prayer, Scripture, obedience drills)*
- **Create** *a crisis response protocol for spiritual turbulence*
- **Lock** *in an accountability partnership ("Co-Pilot Pact")*

RESULT: UNSHAKABLE PREPAREDNESS—EQUIPPED TO HANDLE BOTH SMOOTH FLIGHTS AND SUDDEN STORMS IN YOUR PURPOSE JOURNEY.

PRE-FLIGHT PRAYER:

Spirit of God, expose what weakens my wings and train me to ride Your currents. I surrender my timeline to You.

Pause. Write what comes to mind:

_____

_____

_____

SECTION 1: RESILIENCE TRAINING 〰〰〰〰〰〰〰〰〰〰〰〰〰〰

KEY TRUTH

"Your spiritual muscles grow strongest in life's turbulence" (Isaiah 40:31).

EXERCISE 1: SOAR FUEL

Rank these spiritual habits by impact (1 = most vital):

❏ *Scripture immersion (e.g., Ephesians 6:17)*

❏ *Prayer that prevails (James 5:16)*

❏ *Community connection (Hebrews 10:25)*

❏ *Worship warfare (Psalm 149:6)*

❏ *Sabbath surrender (Exodus 20:8)*

Your Top Three:

1. _____

2. _____

3. _____

EXERCISE 2: CONSISTENCY AUDIT

I struggle with _____

because _____.

To strengthen this, I'll _____
by _____ *[date].*

SECTION 2: FEATHER SHEDDING

KEY INSIGHT

What you won't release becomes ballast.

EXERCISE 3: WEIGHT INVENTORY

Three weights trapping you at low altitude:

1) **Regret:** *I still beat myself up over* _____.
2) **Mindset:** *I believe* _____ *is impossible for me.*
3) **Wound:** *The pain of* _____ *still grounds me.*

EXERCISE 4: HOLY RELEASE

Choose one weight. Complete this prayer:

"Father, I trade my _____ *for Your*
_____ *(Luke 4:18)."*

SECTION 3: WAITING WISDOM

KEY TRUTH

Waiting isn't wasting—it's incubating
(Ecclesiastes 3:11).

EXERCISE 5: SEASON SENSOR

Current Waiting Room: ❑ *Preparation*   ❑ *Testing*   ❑ *Hidden Growth*

God is using this delay to teach me _____.

EXERCISE 6: ACTIVE WAITING

While I wait, I'll:

- *Pray: _____*
- *Prepare: _____*
- *Practice: _____*

SECTION 4: STORM RIDING

KEY INSIGHT

Fear is just wind beneath your wings

EXERCISE 7: FEAR X-RAY

FEAR	PHYSICAL SYMPTOM	LIE IT TELLS
FAILURE	STOMACH KNOTS	"YOU'LL EMBARRASS YOURSELF"

EXERCISE 8: TRUTH TURBINE

For each fear, write a Scripture jetpack:

1) When I fear _____, *I declare*
_____ *(Psalm 27:1).*

2) When I fear _____,
I declare _____.

3) When I fear _____,
I declare _____.

4) When I fear _____,
I declare _____.

SECTION 5: LAUNCH SEQUENCE

KEY DECLARATION

"My wings are battle-tested; my spirit is wind-ready."

EXERCISE 9: SEVEN-DAY IGNITION

This week, I'll:

- *Courage Step:* _____
- *Daily Drill:* _____ *(e.g., Declare Isaiah 40:31 at sunrise)*
- *Accountability Check-In:* _____ *(Name/Date)*

_____
_____
_____
_____

FINAL REFLECTION: FLIGHT PREP MANIFESTO

Sign and post where you'll see it daily:

I commit to:

- *Strengthening my* _____ *(weakest muscle)*
- *Releasing my* _____ *(heaviest weight)*
- *Soaring through* _____ *(biggest fear)*

Signed: _____ *Date:* _____

Witness: _____

NEXT STEPS:

- **Daily:** *Practice your "Daily Drill" from Exercise 9*
- **Weekly:** *Text your witness one turbulence-to-triumph story*
- **Monthly:** *Revisit Section 3 to assess waiting season progress*

CHAPTER 9

Soaring with Purpose

ALIGNING WITH YOUR DIVINE VISION

"Vision is seeing what God sees when
He looks at your life."

INTRODUCTION: YOUR DIVINE FLIGHT PLAN

This chapter will help you:

- **Clarify** *the difference between vision (God's calling) and mission (practical steps)*
- **Identify** *three passions that align with God's Kingdom purpose*
- **Shift** *from consuming to contributing through your gifts*
- **Develop** *a "Purpose Action Plan" with measurable milestones*
- **Activate** *daily habits to stay aligned with your divine assignment*

RESULT: A CLEAR, ACTIONABLE ROADMAP TO LIVE OUT GOD'S PURPOSE WITH CONFIDENCE AND INTENTIONALITY.

PRE-SOAR PRAYER:

Father, strip away every distraction. Show me:
1) *The vision You've planted in me (the WHY)*
2) *The mission before me (the HOW)*
3) *The action required today (the NOW)*

Pause. Write His whispers below:

_____

_____

_____

_____

SECTION 1: VISION VS. MISSION

KEY TRUTH:

Goals are what you pursue—vision is what pursues you.

EXERCISE 1: VISION X-RAY

GOALS I'VE PURSUED	GOD'S DEEPER VISION BEHIND THEM
GET PROMOTED	INFLUENCE WORKPLACES FOR CHRIST

EXERCISE 2: KINGDOM PASSIONS

Three fires in your heart that reflect God's heart:

1) *I burn to see* _____ *transformed.*
2) *I ache over* _____.
3) *I lose track of time when* _____.

Lightbulb Moment: *Circle the passion that scares you most to pursue.*

SECTION 2: TUNING TO DIVINE FREQUENCY

KEY INSIGHT:

God's voice isn't heard—it's recognized.

EXERCISE 3: HOW GOD SPEAKS TO YOU

Check your primary "signal channels":

❑ *Scripture leaps (verses that feel alive)*

❑ *Persistent nudges (recurring thoughts)*

❑ *Circumstantial signs (divine "coincidences")*

❑ *Community confirmation (others' words)*

❑ *Dreams/visions*

Last time God spoke clearly:
He said _____
about _____.

SECTION 3: FROM CLAY TO CONTRIBUTION

KEY TRUTH:

You're not a container—you're a conduit (2 Corinthians 4:7).

EXERCISE 4: CONSUMPTION DETOX

Where are you stuck in consumer mode?
I spend more time _____
than _____.

EXERCISE 5: GIFT DEPLOYMENT

Three ways to start contributing this week:

1) *Use my gift of* _____
to _____.
2) *Serve at* _____
by _____.
3) *Encourage* _____
through _____.

SECTION 4: FAITH IN MOTION

KEY INSIGHT:

Truth unused becomes trivia.

EXERCISE 6: KNOWLEDGE-ACTION GAP

TRUTH I KNOW	WHY I HAVEN'T ACTED	FIRST STEP
PRAYER WORKS	FEAR OF LOOKING FOOLISH	PRAY ALOUD WITH A FRIEND

SECTION 5: YOUR ETERNAL IMPACT MAP

KEY TRUTH:

Direction trumps speed every time.

EXERCISE 7: LIFE COORDINATES

I'm called to impact _____

through _____.

(Example: Business leaders through biblical leadership coaching)

EXERCISE 8: PROGRESS METRICS

How will you measure success?

❑ *Fruit:* _____ *(e.g., lives changed)*

❑ *Faithfulness:* _____ *(e.g., daily obedience)*

❑ *Freedom:* _____ *(e.g., fear overcome)*

FINAL DECLARATION: SOARING MANIFESTO

Sign and post where you'll see it daily:

I align my:

- **Schedule** *with my vision of* _____
- **Resources** *with my mission to* _____
- **Energy** *with my call to* _____

I am not aimless—I am assignment-driven.

Signed: _____ *Date:* _____

Witness: _____

NEXT STEPS:

- **Today:** *Take the first step from Exercise 6.*
- **Weekly:** *Dedicate thirty minutes to vision refinement.*
- **Monthly:** *Review progress with your witness.*

Weathering the Storm

FINDING STRENGTH IN ADVERSITY

"Eagles don't hide from storms—they harness them."

INTRODUCTION: STORM WISDOM

This chapter will help you:

- **Identify** *any current "storm" (challenge, trial, or transition)*
- **Learn** *how to harness adversity for growth instead of fear*
- **Develop** *a "Storm-Proof Mindset" through Scripture and prayer*
- **Create** *a crisis response plan for future challenges*
- **Turn** *struggles into testimonies of resilience*

RESULT: UNSHAKABLE FAITH AND PERSEVERANCE—EQUIPPED TO THRIVE IN LIFE'S TOUGHEST SEASONS.

PRE-STORM PRAYER:

Holy Spirit, teach me to ride Your currents in any storm. Show me:

1) *Where I've been flapping instead of soaring*
2) *The purpose hidden in any trial*
3) *One practical step to rise above it**

Pause. Write His whispers below:

_____

_____

_____

_____

_____

SECTION 1: SOARING IN THE SPIRIT

KEY TRUTH:

Your wings work better when you stop flapping (Zechariah 4:6).

EXERCISE 1: SELF-RELIANCE AUDIT

I've been trying to "flap" through:

- *Area: _____ (e.g., My marriage conflict)*
- *Evidence: _____ (e.g., Lecturing instead of listening)*

EXERCISE 2: SPIRIT-LED TURNING POINT

Describe one time when obeying the Spirit changed everything:

When I listened, He said _____.
The result was _____.

EXERCISE 3: SENSITIVITY TRAINING

Three ways I'll tune into God's voice this week:

❑ *Pause before decisions to ask: "Spirit, what's Your take?"*

❑ *Journal unexpected promptings*

❑ *Test impressions with Scripture*

SECTION 2: STORMS AS STRENGTH TRAINERS

KEY INSIGHT:

The same wind that uproots trees lifts eagles.

EXERCISE 4: PAST STORM GAINS
(Example: Job loss → deeper dependence)

God used _____

to teach me _____.

EXERCISE 5: CURRENT RESISTANCE

OPPOSITION FACED	HIDDEN GIFT
CRITICISM	CLARIFIED MY CALLING

SECTION 3: EAGLE VS. CHICKEN MINDSET

KEY TRUTH:

You can't claim eagle wings while pecking dirt.

EXERCISE 6: EAGLE UPGRADE

In my current storm, I'll shift from:

- *Reacting like a chicken by* _____
- *Responding like an eagle by* _____

EXERCISE 7: EAGLE DECLARATION

I am _____,
designed to _____!
(Example: I am storm-proof, designed to rise above adversity!)

SECTION 4: UNCOMPROMISING INTEGRITY

KEY INSIGHT:

Compromise clips your wings.

EXERCISE 8: PRESSURE POINTS

Three cultural tides pushing me to compromise:
(e.g., Silencing my faith at work)

1) _____
2) _____
3) _____

EXERCISE 9: BOUNDARY BLUEPRINT

I'll guard my integrity by:

- *Saying no to* _____
- *Saying yes to* _____

SECTION 5: THE COST OF SOARING

KEY TRUTH:

Purpose has a price tag—but it's worth the sacrifice.

EXERCISE 10: SACRIFICE INVENTORY

Following my vision has cost me _____
but gained me _____.

EXERCISE 11: PERSEVERANCE PRAYER

Father, when _____ *feels too hard,*
remind me that _____.

SECTION 6: STORM MANUAL

KEY INSIGHT:

Every storm comes with instructions.

EXERCISE 12: CURRENT BATTLE BRIEF

My Storm: _____

God's Purpose: _____

My Three-Step Response:

1. _____
2. _____
3. _____

FINAL DECLARATION: STORM-SOARING MANIFESTO

Sign and post where you'll see it daily:

This storm will not break me—it will make me.

I exchange:
- *Fear for* _____
- *Flapping for* _____
- *Compromise for* _____

Signed: _____ *Date:* _____

Witness: _____

NEXT STEPS:

- **Today:** *Execute your first response step from Exercise 12.*
- **Weekly:** *Text your witness one storm-surfing victory.*
- **Monthly:** *Review growth from past storms.*

WHY THIS VERSION WORKS BETTER:

1) **Stronger Framing:**
   - *"Storm wisdom" replaces generic "adversity"*
   - *"Flapping vs. soaring" visual is memorable*

2) **Deeper DIAGNOSTICS:**
   - *"Self-reliance audit" exposes works-based thinking*
   - *"Pressure points" name specific cultural challenges*

3) **More PRACTICAL:**
   - *Three-step storm response plan (Exercise 12)*
   - *Checkboxes for sensitivity training (Exercise 3)*

4) **MEMORABLE MECHANICS:**
   - *"Eagle declaration" shout prompt*
   - *Tear-out manifesto for daily reinforcement*

5) **THEMATIC CONSISTENCY:**
   - *Every exercise ties to eagle/storm imagery*

Associations

A PATHWAY TO TRANSFORMATION OR DEFORMATION

*"Show me your closest five friends, and
I'll show you your future."*

INTRODUCTION: YOUR RELATIONAL WINDS

This chapter will help you:

- *Evaluate your inner circle's impact on your purpose*
- *Discover the three types of relationships you must have:*
    - ✓ Confidants: Those who sharpen your faith
    - ✓ Constituents: Those who share your mission
    - ✓ Comrades: Those who fuel your joy
- *Test your mentors/influencers like the Bereans (Acts 17:11)*
- *Upgrade your connections with practical steps*

RESULT: A GOD-ALIGNED INNER CIRCLE THAT PROPELS YOU FORWARD.

PRE-REFLECTION PRAYER:

Father, expose any relationship that's clipping my wings. Highlight those who push me toward Your purpose.

Pause. Write impressions below:

_____

_____

_____

_____

SECTION 1: RELATIONAL AUDIT

EXERCISE 1: INNER CIRCLE X-RAY

List your five closest relationships:

1) Name: _____ Role:
_____ (e.g., Accountability partner)
2) Name: _____
Role: _____
3) Name: _____
Role: _____

Answer honestly:

❑ *Who challenges me spiritually? _____*

❑ *Who drains my energy? _____*

❑ *Who knows my God-given vision? _____*

EXERCISE 2: TURBULENCE SOURCES

These relationships create unnecessary storms:

• *Relationship: _____*
  Issue: _____ (e.g., "Criticism")

SECTION 2: BIBLICAL BLUEPRINTS

EXERCISE 3: SCRIPTURAL SPOTLIGHT

SCRIPTURE	HEALTHY ASSOCIATION	WARNING EXAMPLE	YOUR APPLICATION
ACTS 27:22-25	CLARIFIED MY CALLING	N/A	I NEED _____ LIKE PAUL.
1 COR 15:33	N/A	BAD COMPANY	I'LL DISTANCE FROM _____.

SECTION 3: RELATIONAL DISCERNMENT

EXERCISE 4: TRIBE TRIAGE

Categorize your top ten relationships:

#	NAME	ROLE	IMPACT (↑→↓)	ACTION STEP
	JOHN	CONFIDANT	↑ ENCOURAGES	SCHEDULE MONTHLY HIKE
	SARAH	COMRADE	↓ DRAMA	SET BOUNDARIES
1				
2				

#	NAME	ROLE	IMPACT (↑→↓)	ACTION STEP
3				
4				
5				
6				
7				
8				
9				
10				

ROLES DEFINED:

- **Confidant:** *Knows your dreams/prayers*
- **Constituent:** *Supports your work*
- **Comrade:** *Social companion*

SECTION 4: STRATEGIC SHIFTS //

EXERCISE 5: RELATIONAL ACTION PLAN

1) *Elevate: I'll deepen connection with* _____

by _____.

2) *Distance: I'll limit time with* _____

by _____.

3) *Seek: I need a* _____ *(role)*

and will pray for divine connection.

EXERCISE 6: BOUNDARY BLUEPRINT

With _____ *(name), I'll:*

- *Start:* _____ *(e.g., Speaking up about values)*
- *Stop:* _____ *(e.g., "Pretending to agree")*

FINAL DECLARATION: TRIBE MANIFESTO //////////////////////////////////////

Sign and share with one confidant:

I commit to:

- *Investing in* _____ *who sharpen me (Proverbs 27:17)*
- *Releasing* _____ *who distract me*
- *Seeking* _____ *who challenge me*

Signed: _____ *Date:* _____

Witness: _____

NEXT STEPS:

- **This Week:** *Initiate one elevation action*
- **Monthly:** *Review relational impacts*
- **Quarterly:** *Assess new divine connections*

CHAPTER 12

The Eagle's Gaze

DEVELOPING SPIRITUAL PERCEPTION

"Eagles see 8x clearer than humans — how much more should Spirit-filled believers?"

INTRODUCTION: HEAVEN'S PERSPECTIVE

This chapter will help you:

- **Upgrade** *your vision from natural sight to supernatural discernment*
- **Identify** *three areas where you've been viewing life through a limited lens*
- **Activate** *the "Pray First, Move Second" principle in decisions*
- **Develop** *daily habits to sharpen your spiritual focus*

RESULT: A TRANSFORMED PERSPECTIVE THAT SEES CHALLENGES AS OPPORTUNITIES AND ALIGNS EVERY CHOICE WITH GOD'S VISION.

PRE-REFLECTION PRAYER:

Father, lift me above my limited perspective. Show me what You see when You look at my life.

Pause. Write what comes to mind:

_____

_____

_____

_____

SECTION 1: CURRENT VISION CHECKUP

EXERCISE 1: SPIRITUAL EYE CHART
   Rate your clarity (1-5) in these areas:

❑ *Spiritual:* _____ *(Discernment of God's voice)*

❑ *Mental:* _____ *(Kingdom-focused thinking)*

❑ *Emotional:* _____ *(Seeing through faith vs. fear)*

My murkiest area is _____

because _____.

EXERCISE 2: LOT VS. ABRAHAM AUDIT

DECISION FACTOR	LOT'S CHOICE (GEN 13:10-11)	ABRAHAM'S REWARD (GEN 13:14-15)	YOUR PARALLEL
BASIS	WELL-WATERED LAND (NATURAL)	ALL YOU SEE (SUPERNATURAL)	I'VE CHOSEN BASED ON _____.
RESULT	SODOM'S DESTRUCTION	COVENANT BLESSING	THIS LED TO _____.

SECTION 2: DEVELOPING EAGLE VISION ////////////////////////////////

EXERCISE 3: SEEING BEYOND THE SURFACE

Describe when God showed you:
(Example: A job rejection → divine protection)

The reality behind _____
was actually _____.

EXERCISE 4: PRAYER-ALIGNED DECISIONS

CURRENT DECISION	NATURAL OBSERVATION	SPIRITUAL REVELATION
CAREER MOVE	BETTER SALARY	KINGDOM INFLUENCE)

SECTION 3: VISION PROTECTION ////////////////////////////////

EXERCISE 5: INFLUENCE X-RAY

Who in your circle:

↑ *Sharpens your vision:* _____ *(How?)*
↓ *Dulls your sight:* _____ *(How?)*

EXERCISE 6: SCRIPTURE LENSES

Three promises that define your future:

1) _____ *(Verse)*
2) _____
3) _____

SECTION 4: PROPHETIC ACTIVATION

EXERCISE 7: MODERN EAGLE CHALLENGE

"Apostle Ogbonmwan's story confronts my:

❑ *Excuses: "I've said _____."*

❑ *Focus: "I've prioritized _____ over _____."*

❑ *Timing: I've delayed _____ because _____.*

EXERCISE 8: 90-DAY VISION SPRINT

By _____ [date], I will:

- *See differently: _____ (e.g., Journal God's whispers daily)*
- *Act boldly: _____ (e.g., Start that ministry podcast)*

FINAL DECLARATION: VISION MANIFESTO

Sign and post where you'll see it daily:

I exchange:

- *Myopic thinking for* _____ *(Isa 55:9)*
- *Reactive moves for* _____ *(Prov 3:5-6)*
- *Earthly vision for* _____ *(Col 3:2)*

Signed: _____ *Date:* _____

Witness: _____

NEXT STEPS:

- **Today:** *Meditate on one Scripture from Exercise 6.*
- **Weekly:** *Assess decisions using the Prayer-Aligned table.*
- **Monthly:** *Review your Ninety-Day Vision Sprint*

Rise Above the Battle

HOW TO FIGHT LIKE A VICTOR, NOT A VICTIM

*"Eagles don't fight on the ground—
they strike from above."*

INTRODUCTION: THE EAGLE'S WAR MANUAL

This Chapter Will Empower You To:

- **Recognize** *when you're fighting in human strength instead of God's power*
- **Disarm** *Three common enemy tactics attacking your mind*
- **Armor** *Up with specific Scripture weapons for daily battles*
- **Develop** *a warfare prayer strategy that works*

RESULT: UNSHAKABLE SPIRITUAL AUTHORITY TO OVERCOME CHALLENGES FROM A POSITION OF VICTORY, NOT FEAR.

PRE-BATTLE PRAYER:

Father, lift me above this battlefield. Show me how to fight from Your throne room, not the trenches.

Pause. Write what comes to mind:

_____

_____

_____

_____

SECTION 1: YOUR STRATEGIC POSITION

EXERCISE 1: ALTITUDE CHECK (JOB 39:27-29)

I've been fighting _____
from the valley when God says I belong on the Rock.
(Example: My financial fears)

EXERCISE 2: STRENGTH SWAP

BATTLE AREA	MY EFFORTS	GOD'S PROMISE
ANXIETY	OVERTHINKING	PHIL 4:6-7

SECTION 2: ENEMY INTELLIGENCE

EXERCISE 3: LIE INTERCEPTION

The enemy's most-used weapon against me is _____,
making me feel _____.

EXERCISE 4: TRUTH MISSILE

When _____ *(lie) attacks, I counter*
with _____ *(Scripture).*

SECTION 3: MIND RENEWAL

EXERCISE 5: THOUGHT CAPTURE (2 COR 10:5)

RECURRING NEGATIVE THOUGHT	SCRIPTURAL TRUTH	DECLARATION
"I CAN'T DO THIS"	PHIL 4:13	"CHRIST STRENGTHENS ME!"

SECTION 4: SPIRITUAL WARFARE

EXERCISE 6: DECLARATION STRIKE

Based on Romans 8:37, I decree:

"I am more than a conqueror in _____ *.*
No _____ *can separate me from God's love!"*

EXERCISE 7: WORSHIP WEAPON

This week, when _____ *(battle) arises,*
I'll worship by _____ *.*

SECTION 5: VICTORY DEPLOYMENT

EXERCISE 8: TODAY'S BATTLE PLAN

- ❑ *Spiritual: I will pray* _____
  at _____ *(time).*

- ❑ *Mental: I replace* _____
  with _____ *(truth).*

- ❑ *Relational: I'll connect with* _____ *(ally) for accountability.*

EXERCISE 9: EAGLE ALLIES

Who sharpens my vision? _____ *Next step*
to grow this: _____

FINAL DECLARATION: VICTORY MANIFESTO

Sign and post where you'll see it daily:

I fight from victory, not for it.
    My position is _____ *(Eph 2:6).*
    My weapons are _____ *(2 Cor 10:4).*
    My outcome is _____ *(1 John 5:4).*

Signed: _____ *Date:* _____

Witness: _____

NEXT STEPS:

- **Immediate:** *Execute your Battle Plan. (Exercise 8)*
- **Daily:** *Speak your Declaration Strike aloud.*
- **Weekly:** *Text your Eagle Ally one victory.*

CHAPTER 14

Feeding the Eagle Within

STRENGTHENING YOUR SPIRIT AND MIND

"Your diet determines your altitude."

INTRODUCTION: YOU ARE WHAT YOU CONSUME

*"An eagle that eats chicken feed will
never outsoar barnyard birds."*

This chapter will help you:

- **Audit** *your current spiritual diet (what's feeding your mind and soul daily)*
- **Replace** *junk food with holy fuel through practical daily habits*
- **Develop** *a twenty-one-day meal plan for spiritual growth*
- **Guard** *your mental gates against toxic input*

RESULT: A SHARP, STRONG SPIRIT THAT SOARS HIGHER BECAUSE IT'S FED THE RIGHT FOOD.

PRE-REFLECTION PRAYER: %%%

Father, expose every source that's malnourishing my spirit. Give me a hunger for what truly strengthens my wings.

Pause. Write what comes to mind:

_____

_____

_____

_____

SECTION 1: CURRENT DIET SCAN %%%%%%%%%%%%%%%%%%%%%%%%%%%%%%%%%%%%%%%

EXERCISE 1: SPIRITUAL NUTRITION LABEL

My primary faith foods this month:

❑ *Main Course:* _____ *(e.g., Sunday sermons)*

❑ *Snacks:* _____ *(e.g., Instagram devotionals)*

❑ *Supplements:* _____ *(e.g., Worship playlists)*

I spend _____ mins/day in direct Scripture engagement vs. _____ mins consuming secondary sources.

EXERCISE 2: TRUTH VERIFICATION

Recently, I heard _____. When I checked Scripture, I discovered _____.

SECTION 2: FROM FAST FOOD TO FEAST

EXERCISE 3: ENCOUNTER AUDIT

My faith is currently fed by:

- ❑ *Hand-me-downs (others' revelations)*
- ❑ *Leftovers (past encounters)*
- ❑ *Fresh bread (daily manna)*

To shift this, I'll:

1) **Start:** _____ *(e.g., Journaling Scripture prayers)*
2) **Stop:** _____ *(e.g., Scrolling before Bible time)*

EXERCISE 4: INFLUENCE INSPECTION

TOP 3 SPIRITUAL VOICES	BEREAN TEST (ACTS 17:11)	ACTION
PASTOR JOHN	ALWAYS GIVES SCRIPTURE	KEEP
PODCAST X	OFTEN OPINION-HEAVY	LIMIT

SECTION 3: HOLY MEAL PLANNING

EXERCISE 5: DIET UPGRADE

This week's spiritual menu:

Breakfast: _____ *(e.g., "Psalm 143:8 meditation")*
Lunch: _____ *(e.g., "Lunchbreak prayer walk")*
Dinner: _____ *(e.g., "Exodus study before bed")*

EXERCISE 6: GATE GUARDING

I'll filter _____ *(media/habits)*
through _____ *(Scripture).*

SECTION 4: VITAL SIGNS CHECK

EXERCISE 7: FRESH MANNA TEST

My last fresh word from God was about _____.
It changed my _____.

EXERCISE 8: GROWTH MARKERS

Circle current signs:
- *Hunger: Craving deeper truth*
- *Fruit: Others notice Christ in me*
- *Discernment: Spotting counterfeits*

FINAL DECLARATION: EAGLE EATER'S MANIFESTO

Sign and post where you'll see it daily:

I commit to:

- *Consuming* _____ *(primary nutrition)*
- *Fasting from* _____ *(spiritual junk food)*
- *Sharing* _____ *(truth with others)*

Signed: _____ *Date:* _____

Witness: _____

NEXT STEPS:

- **Today:** *Implement one meal from Exercise 5.*
- **Weekly:** *Try a twenty-four-hour "media fast".*
- **Monthly:** *Revisit Growth Markers.*

The Wilderness Experience

YOUR TRAINING GROUND FOR GREATNESS

"No eagle learns to soar in a cage. Your barren place is not abandonment—it's acceleration."

INTRODUCTION: THE WILDERNESS RUNWAY

This chapter will help you:

- **Reframe** *your wilderness season as divine preparation (Deut. 8:2-3)*
- **Identify** *three areas where God is stretching you right now*
- **Develop** *a forty-day resilience plan with daily obedience steps*

RESULT: A TRANSFORMED PERSPECTIVE THAT SEES DIFFICULTY AS TRAINING AND EMERGES SPIRITUALLY STRONGER.

WILDERNESS PRAYER:

Father, show me what You're cultivating in this season. Give me eagle eyes to see beyond the dryness.

Pause. Write what comes to mind:

_____

_____

_____

_____

SECTION 1: WILDERNESS WISDOM /////////////////////////////////////

EXERCISE 1: BIBLICAL CASE STUDIES

LEADER	WILDERNESS	PURPOSE	YOUR PARALLEL
MOSES	MIDIAN DESERT	HUMILITY TRAINING	MY _____ SEASON IS TEACHING ME _____.
DAVID	CAVES	LEADERSHIP PREP	IN MY CAVES, GOD IS _____.

KEY INSIGHT:

God uses wilderness to replace self-reliance with God-dependence.

SECTION 2: PERSONAL WILDERNESS MAP //

EXERCISE 2: STRETCH ZONES

Three areas God is expanding in you:

1) **Character:** _____ *(e.g., Patience)*
2) **Faith:** _____ *(e.g., Trusting provision)*
3) **Calling:** _____ *(e.g., Leadership capacity)*

EXERCISE 3: COMFORT DETOX

God is asking me to release _____ *(comfort) to*
embrace _____ *(calling).*

SECTION 3: WILDERNESS SURVIVAL KIT //

EXERCISE 4: DAILY MANNA PRAYER

Lord, in this season of _____, *teach me to*
rely on Your _____.

EXERCISE 5: SPIRITUAL WEAPONS LOCKER

WILDERNESS CHALLENGE	SCRIPTURE WEAPON	DECLARATION
LONELINESS	DEUT 31:8	"YOU GO BEFORE ME!"

SECTION 4: WILDERNESS PROGRESS TRACKER

THIRTY-DAY RESILIENCE JOURNEY
(Circle daily victories)

Week 1: Foundation

❑ *Day 1: Identified wilderness purpose (Ex. 3:1-12)*

❑ *Day 2: Memorized Isaiah 40:31*

❑ *Day 3: Released one comfort item*

❑ *Day 4: Spoke three gratitude declarations*

Week 2: Engagement

❑ *Day 8: Prayed "Manna Prayer" from Ex. 4*

❑ *Day 9: Journaled God's faithfulness*

❑ *Day 10: Shared encouragement with someone*

Week 3-4: Momentum

❑ *Day 21: Noted character growth*

❑ *Day 30: Celebrated one wilderness win*

FINAL DECLARATION: WILDERNESS MANIFESTO

Sign and post where you'll see it daily:

This wilderness is my training ground.

I exchange:
- *Complaints for* _____ *(Phil 2:14)*
- *Fear for* _____ *(2 Tim 1:7)*
- *Hurry for* _____ *(Hab 2:3)*

Signed: _____ *Date:* _____

Witness: _____

NEXT STEPS:

- **Today:** *Begin Thirty-Day Tracker.*
- **Weekly:** *Review biblical wilderness examples.*
- **Monthly:** *Assess growth markers.*

From Hidden to Heralded

HOW GOD REVEALS WHAT HE REFINED IN SECRET

"God's greatest masterpieces are created in secret before they're unveiled to the world."

INTRODUCTION: THE POWER OF HIDDEN SEASONS

Key Truth:

- *Your hidden season is not abandonment—it's divine incubation (Isaiah 49:2).*
- *God refines before He reveals (Psalm 102:13).*
- *What feels like silence is actually sacred preparation.*

This Chapter Will Help You:

- **Recognize** *signs your "hidden season" is ending*
- **Mine** *three key lessons from your preparation time*
- **Launch** *boldly with a ninety-day visibility plan*

RESULT: CONFIDENCE TO STEP INTO YOUR MOMENT WITH DIVINE TIMING AND ANOINTING.

PRAYER OF PREPARATION:

Father, open my eyes to see the purpose in my hiddenness. Show me what You're refining in me for future revelation.

Pause. Write what comes to mind:

_____

_____

_____

_____

SECTION 1: THE PURPOSE OF HIDDENNESS

EXERCISE 1: BIBLICAL PATTERNS

BIBLICAL FIGURE	HIDDEN SEASON	PURPOSE	YOUR PARALLEL
JOSEPH	PRISON	LEADERSHIP TRAINING	MY _____ IS PREPARING ME FOR _____.
DAVID	FIELDS	CHARACTER DEVELOPMENT	IN MY OBSCURITY, GOD IS _____.

EXERCISE 2: HIDDEN SEASON REFLECTION

1) *I felt most hidden when* _____.
At first, I felt _____,
but now I see _____.
2) *Three lessons from my hidden season:*

- _____
- _____
- _____

SECTION 2: SIGNS OF SHIFT

EXERCISE 3: SEASONAL INDICATORS

Check signs you're experiencing:

- ❏ *Divine discontent (holy dissatisfaction)*
- ❏ *Recurring confirmations (themes in prayer/Scripture)*
- ❏ *Doors cracking open (new opportunities)*
- ❏ *Renewed vision (old dreams resurfacing)*

EXERCISE 4: PRAYER UPGRADE

Shift your prayer focus:
From: "God, get me out!" → *To: "God, prepare me for what's next by. . ."*

(Complete the sentence)

_____

_____

SECTION 3: RESILIENCE REVIEW //

EXERCISE 5: SPIRITUAL MUSCLE CHECK

God has strengthened my:

- _____ *muscle (e.g.,*
  patience) through _____
- _____ *muscle (e.g.,*
  courage) through _____ *

EXERCISE 6: FAILURE FORTIFICATION

My 'failure' in _____ *became my*
foundation for _____.

SECTION 4: STEPPING INTO VISIBILITY //////////////////////////////////////

EXERCISE 7: SMALL BEGINNINGS

This week, I'll take these three steps toward my new season:

1. _____
2. _____
3. _____

EXERCISE 8: HUMILITY GUARDRAILS

I'll stay grounded by:

- *Maintaining* _____ *(spiritual discipline)*
- *Serving in* _____ *(hidden place)*
- *Sharing credit with* _____ *(key supporters)*

SECTION 5: BOLD OBEDIENCE

EXERCISE 9: COURAGE CHALLENGE

God is asking me to:

- ❑ *Start:* _____
- ❑ *Stop:* _____
- ❑ *Step into:* _____ *

EXERCISE 10: WILDERNESS CARRY-OVERS

These hidden-season practices must continue:

- _____
- _____

FINAL DECLARATION: HERALDING MANIFESTO

Sign and declare:

My hidden days were not wasted—they were weaponized.

I carry forward:

- *The* _____ *I learned in silence*
- *The* _____ *forged in obscurity*
- *The* _____ *birthed in waiting*

I step boldly into my heralded season, anchored in humility and armed with divine preparation.

Signed: _____ *Date:* _____

Witness: _____

NEXT STEPS: ///

- **Today:** *Take your first "small beginning" from Ex. 7.*
- **Weekly:** *Review your Spiritual Muscle Check.*
- **Monthly:** *Assess growth with your witness.*

C H A P T E R   1 7

The Majestic Eagle

WELCOME TO YOUR KINGDOM LIVING

Eagles don't strive—they soar. You were born for dominion, not desperation.

INTRODUCTION: YOUR ROYAL CALLING

The exercises in this chapter will help you transition from striving to sovereign living by embracing your royal identity in Christ through practical spiritual disciplines, authentic community, and purposeful legacy-building.

Key Truths:

- *Rest is your birthright (Matthew 11:28-30).*
- *Community is your strength (Ecclesiastes 4:9-12).*
- *Legacy is your responsibility (2 Timothy 2:2).*

This Chapter Will Help You:

- **Implement** *three royal habits (prayer, purpose, praise)*
- **Break** *three chicken-like tendencies (fear, small thinking)*
- **Live** *as an ambassador of heaven everywhere you go*

RESULT: AN UNSHAKABLE IDENTITY THAT INFLUENCES EVERY AREA OF YOUR LIFE.

DECLARATION PRAYER:

Father, awaken me to my royal identity. Teach me to reign in rest, walk in wisdom, and multiply my legacy for Your glory.

Pause. Write what stirs in your spirit:

_____

_____

_____

_____

SECTION 1: RESTING IN ROYALTY

EXERCISE 1: STRIVING ASSESSMENT
(Example: My career → Trust Your provision)

I've been striving in _____ *when You're inviting me to* _____ .

EXERCISE 2: DAILY SANCTUARY PLAN

Design your ideal fifteen-minute "throne room" routine:

Time: _____

Place: _____

Anchor Verse: _____

Posture: _____ *(kneeling/walking/journaling)*

SECTION 2: KINGDOM COMMUNITY

EXERCISE 3: INNER CIRCLE EVALUATION

NAME	ROLE	ACTION TO STRENGTHEN

EXERCISE 4: RELATIONAL GROWTH PLAN

This week, I will:

- *Contact* _____ *to schedule spiritual check-in*
- *Join* _____ *(group/study)*
- *Serve at* _____ *(ministry/event)*

SECTION 3: LEGACY MULTIPLICATION

EXERCISE 5: TESTIMONY STEWARDSHIP

My breakthrough in _____
can help _____
(person/group) by _____.

EXERCISE 6: MENTORING PLAN

Name one person to:

Encourage: _____
(Method: _____ *)*

Develop: _____

(First step: _____ *)*

SECTION 4: DAILY KINGDOM RHYTHMS 〰〰〰〰〰〰〰〰〰〰

EXERCISE 7: PURPOSE DISCIPLINES

My non-negotiables:

Morning: _____

Evening: _____

EXERCISE 8: PURPOSE REFRESH

I'll incorporate _____ *into my week to renew my joy in calling.*

SECTION 5: LIMITLESS LIVING 〰〰〰〰〰〰〰〰〰〰

EXERCISE 9: BARRIER IDENTIFICATION

God is challenging my self-imposed limit of _____ *.*

First step to overcome: _____

EXERCISE 10: BOLD ACTION PLAN

This week's faith step:

I will _____ *at*

_____ *(time/place).*

SECTION 6: AUTHORITY ACTIVATION

EXERCISE 11: DIVINE PROMPTINGS

God is prompting me to:

Start: _____

Stop: _____

Step into: _____

EXERCISE 12: IDENTITY ALIGNMENT

Replace "I can't _____ *" with "I am*
_____ *(Scriptural truth)"*

FINAL DECLARATION: KINGDOM MANIFESTO

Sign and declare daily:

I am a royal heir, called to:

- *Rest in* _____ *(Psalm 91:1)*
- *Reign over* _____ *(Genesis 1:28)*
- *Reproduce* _____ *(Matthew 10:8)*

My eternal impact begins today.

Signed: _____ *Date:* _____

Witness: _____

NEXT STEPS:

- **Immediate:** *Implement one practice from Section 4.*
- **Weekly:** *Complete your Bold Action Plan.*
- **Monthly:** *Review legacy progress.*

CHAPTER 18

Final Charge
The Flight Has Begun

SOAR ABOVE THE NOISE

INTRODUCTION: THE MOMENT OF ASCENSION

This is your divine commissioning. Every lesson learned, every chain broken, every truth embraced has been preparing you for this moment—not to simply admire the skies from below, but to claim them as your rightful domain. Like an eagle sensing the shift in winds, you now stand at the precipice between who you were and who you were reborn to be. This chapter is your launch protocol.

Key Truths:

- *Completion is not an ending but an elevation (Philippians 1:6).*
- *Your past journey has equipped you for future conquests (Romans 8:37-39).*
- *The Kingdom needs your voice in the heavens (Isaiah 40:31).*

This Chapter Will Help You:

- **Synthesize** *your biggest breakthroughs*
- **Confront** *one final barrier holding you back*
- **Launch** *with a signed "Flight Covenant"*

YOUR RESULT: A CLEAR FLIGHT PATH INTO YOUR GOD-GIVEN DESTINY WITH UNSTOPPABLE MOMENTUM.

PRAYER OF COMMISSION: //

Father, as I complete this journey, awaken the eagle's instinct within me. Give me courage to leap when You say leap, to rise when others retreat, and to claim the altitudes You've prepared for me.

Pause. Write the first thing that comes to mind after this prayer:

_____

_____

_____

_____

SECTION 1: IDENTITY AND GROWTH REFLECTION ////////////////////////////////////

EXERCISE 1: TRANSFORMATIONAL INSIGHTS

1) *Through this journey, God has revealed my true identity as* _____.
2) *My most significant growth has been in* _____ *(mindset/faith/ purpose) through* _____.
3) *I've surrendered these limiting beliefs to God:* _____.

SECTION 2: COURAGEOUS OBEDIENCE //

EXERCISE 2: CALLING CLARIFICATION

1) *God is calling me to* _____, *but I've hesitated because* _____.
2) *To obey fully, I must confront these fears:* _____.
3) *My divine accountability partners are:* _____.

SECTION 3: INSPIRATIONAL PARALLELS

EXERCISE 3: STORY APPLICATION

1) From the testimonies, I was most impacted by _____
because _____.
2) Our shared journey elements include: _____.

SECTION 4: 5-STEP SOARING PLAN

Action Plan:

1) Name What's Grounding You
- *The lie:* _____
- *God's truth:* _____ *(Scripture reference)*

2) Spiritual Fuel
- Daily prayer: _____
- Anchor promise: Ephesians 3:14-21 (personalize verse 20)

  _____

3) Immediate Faith Step
- *This week I will:* _____
  by _____ *(date).*

4) Kingdom Community
- *I will connect with* _____ *for*
  accountability by _____ *(date).*

5) Legacy Multiplication
- *I will share* _____
  lesson with _____.

SECTION 5: LIFTOFF COMMITMENT

Final Declaration:

I, _____, *declare that:*

- *My identity is rooted in _____ (Scripture)*
- *My mission is to _____*
- *My daily practice will be _____*

Today's action: _____

CLOSING CHARGE

"The runway ends here. This is your divine moment of lift-off. The skies await your obedience, not your perfection. Where others see turbulence, you will find thermals of grace. Fix your gaze beyond the storm clouds of circumstance to the throne that commissions your flight. Your wings were fashioned for this moment. Leap."

NEXT STEPS:

- *Immediately complete your "Today's action".*
- *Within seven days: Execute your faith step.*
- *Within thirty days: Review progress with your accountability partner.*

You weren't created to watch others soar—
your birthright is the open sky.
The world's noise will try to tether you,
but the wind of the Spirit is calling upward.
So stop measuring your wings.
Stop calculating the risks.
The greatest danger isn't falling—
it's never leaving the ledge.
Take the leap.
Spread your God-given wings.
And discover the breathtaking truth:
You were always meant to soar.
Now—today—
the sky awaits its rightful heir.

—Your fellow sky-dweller
Tessy Tanyi

www.ingramcontent.com/pod-product-compliance
Lightning Source LLC
Chambersburg PA
CBHW080546090426

42734CB00016B/3214